Navigating the Spectrum: Asperger's Syndrome in Adult Women

How to Embrace Your Unique Traits, Overcome Challenges, and Thrive as an Adult Woman with Asperger's Syndrome

Jennifer R. Greger

Copyright © 2023 Jennifer R. Greger

Disclaimer

The information contained in this book is intended for educational and informational purposes only. It is not intended to be a substitute for professional medical advice, diagnosis, or treatment. Always seek the advice of your physician or other qualified healthcare provider with any questions you may have regarding a medical condition. The author and publisher of this book are not responsible for any adverse effects or consequences resulting from the use of any suggestions or procedures described in this book.

DEDICATION

To all the incredible women with Asperger's Syndrome who have navigated the challenges of life with grace and perseverance, this book is for you. May it serve as a guide and a source of inspiration as you continue to embrace your unique traits, overcome obstacles, and thrive in a world that doesn't always understand you.

Table of Contents

INTRODUCTION

As she walked down the crowded street, Helen couldn't help but feel like an outsider. The bustling city, with its constant noise and frenetic pace, seemed to be moving at a different beat than she was. For years, Helen had felt this way - like she didn't quite fit in with the rest of the world. It wasn't until she was in her thirties that she finally discovered why. Helen had Asperger's Syndrome.

As she delved deeper into her diagnosis and began to understand more about her condition, Helen realized that she wasn't alone. Many other women were just like her - navigating the complexities of life on the autism spectrum. And yet, despite the fact that autism was becoming more widely recognized, much of the research and resources available focused primarily on men.

In "Navigating the Autism Spectrum: Asperger's Syndrome in Adult Women," we explore the unique challenges faced by women with Asperger's Syndrome. This book is dedicated to all the adult women who have Asperger's Syndrome, and are looking for ways to live their lives to the fullest.

Asperger's Syndrome is a developmental disorder that affects an individual's social and communication skills, and can impact their behavior and interests. It can be challenging to navigate through life with Asperger's Syndrome, especially for women who are often diagnosed later in life, or not at all.

If you're a woman who has always felt like an outsider, or if you're someone who loves and supports a woman on the autism spectrum, this book is for you. It's a powerful resource for understanding, accepting, and celebrating the unique traits and abilities of women on the autism spectrum.

CHAPTER 1

WHAT IT IS AND HOW IT AFFECTS WOMEN DIFFERENTLY

Asperger's Syndrome is a fascinating neurological condition that affects an individual's ability to communicate, socialize, and interact with others. It is part of the Autism Spectrum Disorder (ASD), and is often referred to as high-functioning autism.

Interestingly, women with Asperger's Syndrome may experience the same challenges as men with the condition, but they often face unique struggles that are not commonly associated with ASD. For instance, women may be better at masking their symptoms in social situations, which can lead to a delayed or misdiagnosis. Women may also have a narrower range of interests and social circles, and may find it challenging to form close friendships.

Understanding the specific challenges that women with Asperger's Syndrome face is crucial in providing effective support and guidance. This chapter will provide a comprehensive overview of the condition, its causes, and how it can impact women differently.

Asperger's Syndrome is caused by a combination of genetic and environmental factors. It is believed to result from abnormalities in brain development, particularly in areas related to social interaction and communication.

Symptoms of Asperger's Syndrome can vary widely but may include difficulties with social interaction and communication, repetitive behaviors or routines, sensory sensitivities, and intense interests in specific topics.

In women, Asperger's Syndrome may manifest in different ways than in men. Women may be better at hiding their symptoms in social situations and may have a better understanding of social cues and etiquette. However, they may also struggle with social anxiety and sensory overload, and find it difficult to form close friendships or maintain romantic relationships.

DIAGNOSING ASPERGER'S SYNDROME IN WOMEN

Once you have a better understanding of Asperger's Syndrome in adult women, the next step is to explore the various approaches to diagnosis and the available treatment options. Diagnosing Asperger's Syndrome in women can be a complex process, as the symptoms can often be masked or camouflaged. It is important to find a healthcare professional who is experienced in diagnosing and treating Asperger's Syndrome in women.

A diagnosis of Asperger's Syndrome can be a double-edged sword. On the one hand, it can provide a sense of relief and understanding for women who have struggled to fit in and make sense of their experiences. On the other hand, it can also be overwhelming and even frightening to receive a diagnosis of a condition that is often misunderstood and stigmatized.

Treatment options for Asperger's Syndrome are varied and depend on the individual's unique needs and challenges. It is important to work with a healthcare professional to develop a treatment plan that is tailored to your specific situation. This may include therapy to address social communication difficulties, occupational therapy to address sensory processing challenges, and medication to manage co-occurring conditions such as anxiety or depression.

It is also important to remember that there is no "cure" for Asperger's Syndrome. Rather, the goal of treatment is to help women with Asperger's Syndrome learn coping strategies and develop skills to better navigate their lives. With the right support and resources, it is possible to lead a fulfilling and rewarding life with Asperger's Syndrome.

By understanding the unique ways that Asperger's Syndrome can affect women, you can begin to identify your own strengths and challenges and develop strategies to overcome them. In the next chapter, we will explore how to identify and embrace your unique traits as an adult woman with Asperger's Syndrome.

MYTHS AND MISCONCEPTIONS

It's important to address some of the myths and misconceptions that surround Asperger's Syndrome. Unfortunately, there are many stereotypes and misunderstandings that can make it difficult for women with this condition to get the support and understanding they need.

One common myth is that only boys and men can have Asperger's Syndrome. This is simply not true. While it's true that more boys are diagnosed with the condition, there are many women who have Asperger's Syndrome as well. The diagnostic criteria for the condition do not vary by gender, so it's important for women to be aware that they too can have this condition.

Another myth is that people with Asperger's Syndrome lack empathy or are unable to understand other people's emotions. While it's true that people with Asperger's Syndrome may have difficulty recognizing and interpreting nonverbal cues such as facial expressions and body language, this does not mean they lack empathy. In fact, many people with Asperger's Syndrome are highly empathetic and deeply caring individuals.

Finally, there is a misconception that people with Asperger's Syndrome are all the same. In reality, the condition can present in many different ways, and each person's experience is unique.

This is why it's so important to seek out individualized support and treatment options that are tailored to your specific needs.

CHAPTER 2

RECOGNIZING YOUR STRENGTHS AS A WOMAN WITH ASPERGER'S SYNDROME

As we discussed in the previous chapter, women with Asperger's Syndrome may face unique challenges. However, it's important to remember that this condition is not all negative. In fact, many women with Asperger's Syndrome have unique strengths that should be celebrated and embraced.

The first step in embracing your unique traits is to identify them. This can be a difficult process, as many women with Asperger's Syndrome may have been told their entire lives that they are "weird" or "different." However, it's important to remember that your differences are what make you special, and can be a source of strength and success.

One common trait among women with Asperger's Syndrome is a strong focus on detail and accuracy. This can be incredibly useful in many careers, including science, engineering, and finance. Women with Asperger's Syndrome may also have a unique ability to think logically and objectively, which can be a valuable asset in problem-solving and decision-making.

Another common trait is a deep interest in specific topics or hobbies. While this may be seen as "obsessive" by some, it can also be a source of passion and expertise. Women with Asperger's Syndrome may excel in fields such as history, art, or music, and may have a unique perspective that allows them to see connections and patterns that others might miss.

It's important to note that not all women with Asperger's Syndrome will have the same strengths. Each individual is unique, and it's important to take the time to identify your own unique strengths and talents.

After recognizing your strengths, the next step is to fully accept and appreciate them. This can prove difficult for some women with Asperger's Syndrome who may experience feelings of self-consciousness or shame regarding their differences. Nonetheless, it's crucial to bear in mind that your unique qualities are what distinguish you and should be recognized and cherished.

One way to embrace your strengths is to find a community of like-minded individuals. This can be online or in person, and can provide a safe and supportive space to share your interests and passions. You may also find it helpful to seek out mentors or role models who share your strengths and can offer guidance and support.

To fully embrace your strengths, it's important to find ways to integrate them into your everyday routine. For instance, if you have a strong passion for history, you could spend time visiting museums or historical landmarks. Similarly, if you have musical talent, you might enjoy playing an instrument or attending concerts. By incorporating your strengths into your daily activities, you can experience a sense of joy and fulfillment in the things that you are passionate about.

Furthermore, it's crucial to keep in mind that your strengths can also serve as a source of inspiration and motivation during challenging times. Instead of focusing on your weaknesses, reminding yourself of your strengths can help you stay positive and driven. By embracing your unique characteristics and celebrating your strengths, you can flourish as an adult woman with Asperger's Syndrome.

EMBRACING SELF-CARE AND WELLNESS

Navigating a world that doesn't always understand our unique needs and perspectives can be tough. But don't worry, you have the power to empower yourself by embracing self-care and wellness.

Taking care of yourself may not always come easy. You might face challenges like sensory overload, social anxiety, or executive functioning difficulties. But by making your health and well-being a priority, you can better manage these obstacles and overcome them.

Keep in mind that self-care takes different forms for different people. Some might find tranquility in calm activities like reading or knitting, whereas others may prefer more dynamic activities such as hiking or yoga. It is crucial to dedicate some time each day to take care of yourself, to replenish your energy and concentrate on what is important.

As you immerse yourself in self-care and wellness, you will begin to see yourself and your exceptional qualities in a fresh way. You will start to acknowledge your differences as strengths, not shortcomings, and celebrate your distinctiveness. Through taking care of yourself, you will lead a happier, healthier, and more rewarding life.

CHAPTER 3

COPING STRATEGIES FOR DAILY LIFE

One of the most common challenges faced by individuals with Asperger's Syndrome is sensory overload. This can occur due to loud noises, bright lights, strong smells, or other environmental factors. To manage sensory overload, it is important to identify the specific triggers that cause it and develop coping strategies to deal with them.

One effective coping strategy is to create a calming environment. This can involve reducing clutter in your living space, using soft lighting, and playing soothing music. It is also important to schedule regular breaks throughout the day to give your brain a chance to rest and recover.

Another strategy is to use sensory tools, such as earplugs or noise-canceling headphones, to reduce the impact of environmental triggers. This can be particularly helpful in noisy or crowded environments, such as public transportation or busy shopping centers.

Individuals with Asperger's Syndrome may face difficulties with executive functioning, including planning, organization, and time management, in addition to sensory overload. To tackle these challenges, establishing routines and maintaining a structured schedule can be beneficial. Breaking down tasks into smaller, more manageable steps and using visual aids like calendars or to-do lists can help stay on track.

Stress management is also a key factor to prioritize, which may include relaxation techniques such as deep breathing or meditation, engaging in regular physical activity or exercise, and seeking support from loved ones or mental health professionals if required.

COPING WITH REJECTION AND BULLYING

Above all else, it's crucial to keep in mind that rejection or bullying is not a reflection of your self-worth or value. Although it may be tempting to take negative comments or actions to heart, it's important to recognize that the person or people responsible for the rejection or bullying are the ones with the problem, not you.

It's heartbreaking to feel rejected or bullied by others, and it can take a significant emotional toll on you. You may feel lost, alone, and helpless, but you don't have to go through it alone. Reaching out for help can be an incredibly brave and empowering act. Your support system can comprise people such as friends, family members, or a professional therapist who can help you navigate through your emotions and offer a non-judgmental ear to listen to your experiences.

In addition, seeking out support groups for individuals with Asperger's Syndrome or similar communities where you can find acceptance and understanding can be invaluable. These groups offer a safe space to discuss your struggles and find common ground with others who share similar experiences, making it easier to cope with the challenges you may face.

To manage rejection or bullying, it's crucial to concentrate on your strengths and passions. Participate in activities that bring you happiness and a sense of achievement, and surround yourself with individuals who respect and accept you for who you are. This approach can help you develop self-assurance and toughness when dealing with negative situations.

Keep in mind that you have the authority to establish limits and remove yourself from unhealthy situations. If you're experiencing bullying, document the behavior and report it to a trustworthy authority figure or organization. Don't be afraid to seek assistance and take steps to safeguard yourself.

CHAPTER 4

NAVIGATING PREGNANCY AND CHILDBIRTH

Navigating pregnancy and childbirth can be a unique and challenging experience for any woman, and this is no different for an Asperger mom. As someone with Asperger syndrome, you may have certain traits and characteristics that make this experience more challenging than it would be for a neurotypical mother. However, with the right support and strategies in place, you can successfully navigate this journey and emerge on the other side as a strong and capable mother.

One of the key challenges that you may face during pregnancy and childbirth is sensory overload. As someone with Asperger syndrome, you may be more sensitive to certain stimuli, such as bright lights, loud noises, and strong smells. This can make the experience of giving birth in a hospital setting overwhelming and stressful. To manage this, it may be helpful to work with your healthcare provider to create a sensory-friendly birth plan. This might include things like using dimmer lighting, playing calming music, and avoiding strong smells.

Another challenge that you may encounter is social anxiety. Pregnancy and childbirth often involve a lot of social interaction with healthcare providers, family members, and friends. This can be stressful and overwhelming for someone with Asperger syndrome, who may struggle with social communication and interaction. To manage this, it may be helpful to communicate your needs and preferences with your support system ahead of time. This can include things like asking for more one-on-one time with your healthcare provider, having a designated support person with you during appointments, or even communicating through written or visual communication aids.

Finally, as an Asperger mom, you may also experience challenges with bonding with your baby. This is not uncommon for mothers with Asperger syndrome, who may struggle with emotional regulation and social connection.

However, with support and practice, you can develop a strong and loving bond with your child. This might involve seeking out support from a therapist or support group, practicing sensory activities with your baby, or even communicating through visual aids like photos and videos.

In conclusion, navigating pregnancy and childbirth as an Asperger mom may have its challenges, but with the right support and strategies in place, you can overcome them and emerge as a confident and capable mother. By communicating your needs and preferences, practicing self-care, and seeking out support when needed, you can create a positive and rewarding experience for both yourself and your baby.

Understanding Your Child's Needs and Perspective

As a parent with Asperger syndrome, it can be challenging to understand the needs and perspective of your neurotypical child. You may find it difficult to relate to their emotions or understand their social cues, which can cause frustration and miscommunication in your relationship. However, it is essential to make an effort to understand your child's needs and perspective to ensure a healthy and happy parent-child relationship.

To start, it's crucial to acknowledge that your child's experience may be different from yours. They may have different social expectations or sensory needs that you don't have. Take the time to listen to your child and observe their behavior to gain insight into what they need from you as a parent. You can also seek support from other parents, educators, or professionals to learn more about your child's neurotypical development and how you can best support them.

Communication is key when it comes to understanding your child's needs and perspective. Try to be open and honest with your child about your own struggles and ask them to share their experiences with you as well. This can help create a sense of mutual understanding and trust in your relationship.

Additionally, make an effort to engage in activities that your child enjoys, even if they may not be your own interests. This can help you bond with your child and learn more about their perspective. Remember that it's okay to make mistakes and that parenting is a learning process. With patience and effort, you can build a strong and healthy relationship with your neurotypical child.

NAVIGATING SOCIALIZATION AND PLAYTIME

To navigate socialization and playtime with your child, it's essential to take the time to observe and understand their interests and behaviors. This will help you engage with them in ways that are meaningful to them, while also helping them develop important social skills.

You can also work on building a supportive and nurturing relationship with your child, which can help them feel more comfortable and secure in social situations. This can involve setting aside dedicated time for one-on-one play and conversation, and being patient and understanding when your child may struggle or exhibit behaviors that may be challenging for you to interpret or respond to.

Each child is unique, and there is no one-size-fits-all approach to socialization and playtime. By embracing your child's individuality and finding ways to connect with them on their level, you can help them develop the social skills they need to thrive, while also building a strong and supportive relationship that will last a lifetime.

CASE STUDY 1

Meet Jane (name changed for privacy), a mother who was diagnosed with Asperger's Syndrome while pregnant with her second child. Jane has always had difficulty with sensory issues, and her diagnosis helped her find ways to cope with these challenges. She invested in ear defenders, noise-canceling earplugs, a glide chair, and soft textures around the house to make things more comfortable for her.

Despite these tools, Jane still experiences meltdowns, making her realize that she has much more to learn. She is particularly interested in socializing, as she finds it challenging to interact with other moms while caring for a crying baby. She admits to trying and failing to bond with other moms and finding it exhausting to attend baby groups, such as baby massage classes, baby swim classes, and rhyme time.

Although Jane struggled to connect with other moms, her little boy, who is quite sociable, seemed to enjoy these activities. He goes to a childminder and is popular among his friends, and he has no problem going up to groups of children he doesn't know and trying to play alongside them.

Jane does not want her son to miss out on these experiences, but she finds it difficult to manage the social aspects of these events.

As a mother with Asperger's Syndrome, Jane's story highlights the importance of embracing her unique strengths and challenges while navigating parenting. Although she may struggle with socializing and sensory issues, she recognizes the importance of providing social experiences for her child and finding ways to make it work for her. By understanding her needs and abilities, Jane can provide the best care for her children and embrace parenting in her unique way.

CHAPTER 5

The transition into motherhood can be overwhelming and daunting. It's important to understand that the unique challenges of motherhood with Asperger's Syndrome are real, and they require a different approach to manage them properly.

One of the significant challenges for women with Asperger's is managing the home properly. A well-organized and structured routine can be beneficial in managing daily tasks and responsibilities. It's essential to create a list of daily activities and prioritize them according to their importance. By doing this, you can manage your time effectively, which can help in reducing stress and anxiety levels.

Pregnancy can be an emotional rollercoaster, and for women with Asperger's, it can be especially challenging to navigate. The physical changes and the influx of emotions can be overwhelming, leading to anxiety and sensory overload. It's essential to communicate your feelings to your partner or a trusted friend to help you manage the emotions better.

As you move into motherhood, it's important to develop a strong support system. This can include friends, family, or a support group specifically for women with Asperger's. It's also essential to learn how to delegate responsibilities to others and not be afraid to ask for help. Taking care of yourself is critical during this period, and it's important to set aside some time for yourself to recharge and rejuvenate.

Managing motherhood with Asperger's Syndrome is a challenging task that requires a different approach. By implementing structure and organization, effective time management, developing a strong support system, and taking care of yourself, you can navigate this journey with confidence and grace.

EXPLORING THE POTENTIAL OF ASPERGER'S SYNDROME IN YOUR PARTNER OR CHILDREN

As you observe your partner or children, you may notice certain behaviors or traits that seem different from others. You may see that they struggle with social interactions, have difficulty understanding sarcasm or jokes, or have intense interests in specific topics.

If you suspect that your loved one may have Asperger's, it can be a challenging and emotional journey. You may feel overwhelmed, worried, or unsure about how to approach the situation.

The first step is to seek a professional diagnosis from a qualified healthcare provider. This can help you better understand your loved one's needs and develop a plan to support them.

As you navigate this journey, it's important to remember that everyone is different and may require different types of support. Some individuals with Asperger's may benefit from social skills training or therapy, while others may need support with executive functioning or sensory processing.

You can also help your loved one by creating a safe and accepting environment at home. This means being patient, understanding, and supportive of their unique needs and challenges. It may also mean advocating for their needs in school, at work, or in the community.

Above all, remember that your loved one with Asperger's is still the same person you know and love, and they have unique strengths and talents that make them special. With your love and support, they can thrive and live a fulfilling life.

EMBRACING YOUR STRENGTHS AS A MOTHER WITH ASPERGER SYNDROME

It can be challenging to focus on your strengths, especially when society often highlights your weaknesses. However, by embracing your unique strengths, you can become the best version of yourself and provide the best possible care for your child.

One of the strengths that Asperger's mothers often possess is the ability to hyperfocus. This means that you can concentrate on a task for extended periods, and this trait can be an advantage in caring for your child. You can use your hyperfocus to research parenting techniques, prepare meals, or organize schedules effectively.

Another strength is the ability to be highly observant. As an Asperger's mother, you may notice details that others may not. This skill can help you detect changes in your child's behavior, understand their emotional needs, and react promptly to their needs.

Finally, Asperger's mothers often possess a high level of honesty and directness. You can use this strength to communicate with your child in a straightforward and transparent way. Children appreciate straightforward communication, and it can help build trust and mutual respect between you and your child.

Embracing these strengths as a mother with Asperger's syndrome can be empowering and help you develop a positive self-image. It can also help you build a strong and meaningful relationship with your child.

Allow me to introduce you to Lisa, a mother who always felt like an outsider among other mothers, but it wasn't until she discovered she had Asperger's syndrome that she understood why. Lisa already had an adult daughter, Emily, when she learned of her condition. Motherhood was an uphill battle for Lisa, but after receiving her diagnosis, she gained a better understanding of herself and was able to strengthen her relationship with her daughter.

When Lisa told Emily about her condition, Emily was hesitant at first. But as Lisa explained more about Asperger's and its common traits, Emily recognized particular instances when Lisa's behavior matched up with autism. As they talked more, Emily's relief grew as an AS diagnosis could clarify a lot of baffling behavior for both the person with Asperger's and their loved ones.

One of the pivotal moments for Lisa occurred when Emily asked her if she had any emotions. This query made Lisa realize that she had not said "I love you" to Emily in 24 years. Lisa had always found it challenging to express her feelings to her daughter, but she wanted Emily to know that she loved her. Even though Lisa's emotions might have been different from those of a typical mother, she was positive that she loved her daughter.

Lisa's path to motherhood was unique and not without obstacles. She encountered specific challenges that made parenting more challenging, including sensory overload and social interaction issues that hindered her ability to parent effectively. She felt inadequate at times. There were days when Lisa felt like she was going to lose her mind if Emily didn't stop crying.

On one occasion, Lisa found herself standing in the dining room, crying uncontrollably and repeatedly banging her head against the wall. If you've ever witnessed an autistic child's meltdown, Lisa's behavior would have looked similar. However, her husband, who was watching her, helped her remain grounded in reality, allowing her to stay connected to Emily when she wanted to withdraw.

Despite the obstacles she faced, Lisa treasured her role as a mother to her young child. Having Asperger's Syndrome gave her a distinct childlike perspective, one that never waned. Sharing in her child's exploration of the world rekindled Lisa's appreciation for life through her child's eyes, bringing an exhilarating adventure each day. Although taking care of a newborn was challenging for Lisa, she discovered it became easier to relate to her daughter as she grew older. Lisa learned to embrace motherhood with Asperger's, acknowledging her unique strengths and limitations.

CHAPTER 6

BUILDING MEANINGFUL RELATIONSHIPS WITH FAMILY, FRIENDS, AND CO-WORKERS

One of the most significant challenges faced by individuals with Asperger's Syndrome is navigating social interactions. This can include difficulty understanding social cues, interpreting nonverbal communication, and building and maintaining relationships.

To overcome these challenges, it is important to develop social skills and strategies that can help you connect with others more effectively. This can involve seeking out social skills training programs, reading books or articles on social skills development, and practicing social interactions with friends or family members.

It is also important to find ways to build and maintain social connections that align with your unique interests and strengths. This can involve joining clubs or organizations that focus on your hobbies or passions, attending social events that cater to your interests, or connecting with others online through social media or online communities.

In addition to building new relationships, it is also important to maintain existing ones. This can involve making an effort to stay in touch with friends and family members, being open and honest about your needs and boundaries, and seeking support when needed.

In the end, it's crucial to put self-acceptance and self-compassion first. This means acknowledging and embracing your distinct characteristics and talents, commemorating your achievements, and altering your perspective to view difficulties as chances to develop and advance.

DEVELOPING SOCIAL SKILLS AND COMMUNICATION STRATEGIES

Developing social skills and communication strategies can be challenging for individuals with Asperger's Syndrome, but it's not impossible. With consistent effort and practice, you can improve your social interactions and develop effective communication strategies. Below are the steps that can assist you in initiating:

Step 1: Identify areas of difficulty

The first step in developing social skills and communication strategies is to identify areas where you struggle. Do you have difficulty initiating conversations or maintaining eye contact? Do you struggle to understand nonverbal cues or to express your thoughts clearly? Identifying your areas of difficulty can help you focus your efforts on the areas that need the most attention.

Step 2: Set realistic goals

I know it can be challenging to identify areas where you struggle, but it's an important step in your personal growth journey. Once you've identified those areas, it's time to set some goals for yourself. Keep in mind to be compassionate towards yourself and set practical goals that you can accomplish. Doing so will keep you satisfied and motivated of your accomplishments.

Step 3: Practice, practice, practice

Developing social skills and communication strategies requires practice. Look for opportunities to practice your skills, such as attending social events or joining a social skills group. Practice your skills in a safe, supportive environment and be willing to make mistakes and learn from them.

Step 4: Learn from others

Observe and learn from others who have strong social skills. Watch how they initiate and maintain conversations, use nonverbal cues, and express themselves. You can also seek feedback from friends or family members on your social interactions.

Step 5: Use visual aids

Visual aids, such as diagrams or pictures, can be helpful in understanding social situations and nonverbal cues. For example, you can create a diagram of different facial expressions and what they mean to help you better understand nonverbal cues.

Step 6: Seek professional help

If you're struggling to develop social skills and communication strategies on your own, consider seeking professional help. A therapist or social skills group can provide you with guidance and support as you work to improve your social interactions.

Don't be discouraged if improving your social skills and communication strategies takes time and effort. Remember that progress is possible with consistent practice and the right support. By putting in the work, you can improve your relationships and social interactions, which can lead to a more fulfilling and satisfying life. Stay hopeful and keep striving towards your goals.

Overall, navigating Asperger's Syndrome as an adult woman can be challenging, but it is important to remember that with the right strategies and support, it is possible to embrace your unique traits, overcome challenges, and thrive in all areas of life.

CHAPTER 7

UNDERSTANDING YOUR OWN EMOTIONS AND
RESPONDING TO OTHERS

When we think of empathy, we often imagine it as the ability to put ourselves in someone else's shoes. We picture ourselves feeling their emotions as if they were our own. But empathy is much more than that. It is a complex and multifaceted ability that requires us to understand, regulate, and express our emotions in a way that allows us to connect with others on a deeper level.

For individuals with Asperger's Syndrome, empathy can be a particularly challenging area. The emotional regulation and expression difficulties often experienced can result in social misunderstandings and communication difficulties. However, with a deeper understanding of empathy and emotional regulation, individuals with Asperger's Syndrome can learn to navigate social situations more effectively and develop more meaningful relationships with others.

The first step in exploring empathy is understanding our own emotions. Emotions are complex and often hard to decipher, especially for those with Asperger's Syndrome. However, recognizing and labeling our emotions can be incredibly helpful in regulating them and expressing them appropriately. Mindfulness practices, such as meditation, can also be effective tools in developing emotional awareness.

Once we have a better understanding of our own emotions, we can begin to explore the emotions of others. This involves recognizing and interpreting the emotional cues expressed by others, such as facial expressions, tone of voice, and body language. It also requires us to be able to take the perspective of others, to understand their thoughts and feelings, and to respond in a way that is appropriate to the situation.

One of the keys to developing empathy is practicing active listening. Active listening involves not just hearing the words someone is saying but truly understanding their perspective and emotions. This requires us to put aside our own preconceptions and biases and to truly focus on the other person.

Another important aspect of empathy is emotional regulation. Emotional regulation involves the ability to recognize our own emotional responses and to manage them in a way that is appropriate to the situation. This can involve strategies such as deep breathing, mindfulness, and cognitive reappraisal.

Finally, empathy involves being able to express our emotions in a way that is appropriate to the situation and that allows us to connect with others on a deeper level. This can involve using appropriate body language and tone of voice, as well as being able to share our own experiences and emotions in a way that is relatable to others.

In conclusion, exploring empathy and emotional regulation is a crucial component of navigating Asperger's Syndrome as an adult woman. By developing a deeper understanding of our own emotions and those of others, we can learn to navigate social situations more effectively and develop more meaningful relationships with others. Through mindfulness practices, active listening, and emotional regulation techniques, individuals with Asperger's Syndrome can develop the skills necessary to thrive in a world that can often feel overwhelming and confusing.

COPING WITH ANXIETY AND DEPRESSION

One of the first steps in coping with anxiety and depression is to identify your triggers. What situations or events tend to make you feel anxious or depressed? Once you know your triggers, you can work on developing coping strategies to help you manage those feelings. It may be helpful to keep a journal to track your emotions and identify patterns in your mood.

Another important aspect of managing anxiety and depression is to practice self-care. This means taking care of your physical and emotional needs, such as getting enough sleep, eating a balanced diet, and engaging in activities that bring you joy and relaxation. It's also important to seek out support from loved ones or a therapist who can help you navigate your emotions and provide a safe space to process your feelings.

Emotional regulation skills are also crucial in managing anxiety and depression. This involves learning how to recognize and regulate your emotions in a healthy way. Some strategies to try include deep breathing exercises, meditation, or engaging in physical activity. It's also important to practice self-compassion and give yourself permission to feel your emotions without judgment.

DEALING WITH MELTDOWNS AND SHUTDOWNS

Dealing with meltdowns and shutdowns can be tough for anyone, but for those with Asperger's Syndrome, it can be especially challenging. These emotional responses can be triggered by a variety of factors, such as changes in routine or overwhelming social situations, and can be intense to handle.

The good news is that there are steps you can take to manage these emotional reactions. One important first step is to identify the early warning signs that a meltdown or shutdown might be on the horizon. This could be physical symptoms like sweating or a racing heartbeat, or emotional cues like irritability or anxiety. Recognizing these signs can help you prevent the situation from escalating.

To manage these reactions, practicing self-care and stress reduction techniques can be highly effective. This could include deep breathing exercises, meditation, or physical exercise. These practices can help regulate your emotions and reduce stress levels, making it less likely for a meltdown or shutdown to occur.

Another helpful strategy is to have a plan in place for when these emotional responses occur. This might involve finding a quiet place to relax, engaging in a calming activity, or taking a break from the situation. Having a trusted friend or family member who can support you during these moments can also be a valuable asset.

If you find that you're experiencing frequent meltdowns or shutdowns, it's important to seek professional support. A mental health professional can help you develop personalized strategies for managing your emotions and reducing the frequency and intensity of these reactions.

CHAPTER 8

FINDING PASSION AND PURPOSE IN YOUR HOBBIES AND CAREER

As a woman with Asperger's Syndrome, you may have discovered that you have a unique way of approaching your interests and hobbies. In fact, you may have found that certain activities and topics are more than just hobbies – they are passions that bring joy and meaning to your life. These "special interests" can play an important role in helping you find purpose in both your personal and professional life.

But what exactly are special interests, and how can you use them to your advantage? In this chapter, we'll explore the concept of special interests and their potential impact on your life. We'll also discuss ways to cultivate your passions and integrate them into your career and personal goals.

WHAT ARE SPECIAL INTERESTS?

Special interests are a common trait among individuals with Asperger's Syndrome. They are defined as intense and specific areas of interest that captivate a person's attention and bring them pleasure. These interests often begin in childhood and may continue throughout a person's life. In some cases, special interests can lead to exceptional abilities and even career opportunities.

Special interests can take many forms. For some, it may be a particular academic subject such as history or science. For others, it may be a specific hobby such as painting, music, or sports. Whatever the interest, it is characterized by a deep level of knowledge, enthusiasm, and engagement.

Special interests can be a source of joy, creativity, and personal fulfillment. They can also serve as a pathway to discovering your life's purpose. By pursuing your passions, you may uncover hidden talents and abilities that you never knew you had. You may also find that your interests provide a sense of meaning and direction that can guide your personal and professional goals.

So how can you cultivate your special interests and use them to your advantage? Here are a few tips:

1. **Embrace your interests:** Don't be ashamed or afraid to pursue your passions. Embrace them wholeheartedly and let them bring you joy and fulfillment.

2. **Expand your knowledge:** Read books, take classes, and connect with others who share your interests. The more you learn, the more you can deepen your understanding and appreciation of your passions.

3. **Use your interests as a creative outlet:** Whether it's through writing, art, or music, your special interests can serve as a powerful outlet for your creativity and self-expression.

4. **Look for ways to integrate your interests into your career:** Consider how your interests might be relevant to your career goals. Are there ways to use your passions to enhance your work or pursue new opportunities?

5. **Use your interests as a source of motivation**: When faced with challenges or setbacks, turn to your special interests for inspiration and motivation. They can remind you of the joy and purpose that comes from pursuing what you love.

Special interests offer a range of benefits, both personal and professional. Here are just a few:

1. **Increased motivation:** Pursuing your passions can give you a sense of purpose and direction that can motivate you in all areas of your life.

2. **Enhanced creativity**: Special interests provide a creative outlet that can spark new ideas and ways of thinking.

3. **Improved social connections:** Sharing your interests with others can help you connect with like-minded individuals and build relationships.

4. **Career opportunities:** Special interests can lead to career opportunities in related fields, or even inspire you to start your own business or pursue entrepreneurship.

In conclusion, special interests can play an important role in your life as a woman with Asperger's Syndrome. They offer a unique source of joy, creativity, and personal fulfillment, and can even lead to career opportunities.

EXPLORING CREATIVE OUTLETS AND HOBBIES

One of the most exciting parts of exploring your unique interests and creativity is finding new outlets for self-expression. Whether it's painting, writing, music, or even coding, creative hobbies can be a powerful tool for processing emotions and connecting with the world around you.

When you engage in a creative activity, you have the opportunity to explore your thoughts and feelings in a way that may not be possible through traditional communication. You can experiment with different techniques and styles, pushing the boundaries of what you thought was possible and discovering new aspects of yourself in the process.

Not only is creativity a powerful tool for personal growth and self-discovery, but it can also be a great way to connect with others who share your interests. Joining a writing group, taking a dance class, or attending a pottery workshop can provide opportunities to connect with like-minded individuals, build new friendships, and explore your creative potential in a supportive and collaborative environment.

Of course, it's important to remember that creative pursuits should always be pursued for their own sake, rather than as a means to an end. Whether you're creating for yourself or sharing your work with others, it's important to approach your hobbies with a sense of joy and curiosity, embracing the unique perspectives and approaches that come naturally to you.

So don't be afraid to try new things, explore your passions, and express yourself in ways that feel authentic and true to who you are. With creativity as your guide, the possibilities are truly endless!

EMBRACING UNCONVENTIONAL PERSPECTIVES AND APPROACHES

As someone with Asperger's Syndrome, you may have a unique perspective on the world that sets you apart from others. Your way of thinking and approach to problem-solving may not always fit within the traditional mold, but that doesn't mean it's not valuable.

In fact, embracing your unconventional perspectives and approaches can be a powerful tool for creativity and innovation. Rather than trying to force yourself into a predetermined mold, you can embrace your unique way of thinking and use it to your advantage.

One way to do this is to explore your passions and interests. Maybe you have a deep love for a particular subject or hobby that others don't understand or appreciate. Instead of trying to fit in with what's considered "normal," embrace your unique interests and use them as a source of inspiration and motivation.

It's also important to surround yourself with people who appreciate and support your unconventional perspectives. Seek out like-minded individuals who share your passions and can offer a non-judgmental ear when you need to bounce ideas off someone.

Ultimately, embracing your unconventional perspectives and approaches can be a source of empowerment and fulfillment. Don't let society's expectations hold you back from exploring your creativity and unique way of thinking.

CHAPTER 9

SEEKING SUPPORT AND ACCOMMODATIONS IN THE WORKPLACE AND BEYOND

As an adult with Asperger's Syndrome, navigating the workplace and other environments can be challenging. You may experience difficulty with communication, sensory overload, and social interactions, among other things. However, with the right support and accommodations, you can overcome these challenges and thrive in your personal and professional life. In this chapter, we will discuss the importance of advocating for yourself and seeking support and accommodations to help you succeed.

The first step in advocating for yourself is to understand your strengths and challenges. As a person with Asperger's Syndrome, you may have exceptional abilities in certain areas, such as attention to detail, problem-solving, and pattern recognition. At the same time, you may experience challenges in areas such as communication, social interactions, and sensory processing. By identifying your strengths and challenges, you can better communicate your needs and advocate for accommodations that will help you succeed.

One effective way to advocate for yourself is to work with a professional, such as a therapist or career counselor, who specializes in supporting individuals with Asperger's Syndrome. A professional can help you identify your strengths and challenges and provide guidance on how to communicate your needs effectively. They can also help you navigate the workplace and other environments by providing strategies for managing sensory overload, social interactions, and communication.

Another important aspect of advocating for yourself is understanding your legal rights. Under the Americans with Disabilities Act (ADA), employers are required to provide reasonable accommodations to employees with disabilities, including Asperger's Syndrome. Reasonable accommodations can include modifications to your work environment, such as providing noise-cancelling headphones or adjusting lighting, as well as changes to work processes or duties, such as allowing for flexible scheduling or providing written instructions.

To advocate for accommodations in the workplace, it is important to communicate clearly with your employer. Start by identifying the specific accommodations you need and explaining why they are necessary for you to succeed. Be prepared to provide documentation from a professional, such as a therapist or medical doctor, to support your request. It is also important to emphasize how the accommodations will benefit not only you but also your employer, such as by improving your productivity or reducing workplace stress.

Advocating for yourself can also extend beyond the workplace. For example, you may need accommodations in educational settings or in social situations. In these cases, it is important to communicate your needs clearly and assertively. Be prepared to explain how the accommodations will help you succeed and how they can benefit others in the same situation.

Finally, it is important to remember that self-advocacy is an ongoing process. As you encounter new situations, you may need to advocate for yourself in new ways. By staying informed, building a support network, and communicating your needs clearly, you can successfully navigate the challenges of Asperger's Syndrome and achieve your personal and professional goals.

In conclusion, advocating for yourself is a critical part of navigating Asperger's Syndrome as an adult woman. By understanding your strengths and challenges, working with professionals, understanding your legal rights, and communicating your needs effectively, you can access the support and accommodations you need to succeed in the workplace and beyond. Remember to stay informed, build a support network, and be assertive in communicating your needs. With these strategies, you can thrive as an adult woman with Asperger's Syndrome.

CONNECTING WITH AUTISM AND ASPERGER'S COMMUNITIES

You may feel hesitant or unsure about reaching out, but connecting with others who understand what you're going through can be a game-changer. These communities can offer a wealth of knowledge, resources, and support, as well as a sense of belonging and acceptance that can be hard to find elsewhere.

So, how do you go about connecting with these communities? There are many ways to get involved, depending on your preferences and comfort level. You can start by exploring online forums, social media groups, or local support groups in your area. These communities can provide a safe and welcoming space to share your experiences, ask questions, and connect with others who understand what you're going through.

It can also be helpful to attend events or conferences related to autism or Asperger's Syndrome. These gatherings can be a great way to meet new people, learn about the latest research and developments in the field, and connect with others who share your interests.

Remember, it's okay to take things at your own pace and find the approach that works best for you.

CHAPTER 10

STRATEGIES FOR MAINTAINING AUTONOMY AND BUILDING RELATIONSHIPS

Navigating Asperger's Syndrome can be a challenging journey, especially when it comes to balancing independence and dependence. For many women with Asperger's, it can be difficult to maintain autonomy while building meaningful relationships with others. In this chapter, we will explore strategies that can help you strike a balance between independence and dependence, allowing you to maintain your sense of self while also cultivating meaningful connections with others.

As someone with Asperger's, you may have a natural inclination towards independence. You may feel most comfortable when you are in control of your environment and your schedule. However, independence can also come at a cost. When we focus too much on our own needs and desires, we can unintentionally push others away. It's important to remember that relationships are a two-way street, and that building strong connections with others requires a certain level of interdependence.

So how can you strike a balance between independence and dependence? It's incredible to realize that you have unique strengths that make you special and set you apart from others. Focusing on these strengths, you can build confidence in yourself and your abilities, which can in turn make it easier to connect with others.

Another strategy is to practice empathy. One thing you can do that can really make a difference is to try to see things from the other person's perspective. This can be challenging for someone with Asperger's, as social cues and nonverbal communication can be difficult to interpret. However, by making an effort to understand others' feelings and needs, you can build stronger, more meaningful relationships.

Setting boundaries is also crucial for your emotional wellbeing. While independence is important, it's also important to recognize when you need help or support from others. This can be particularly challenging for someone with Asperger's, as asking for help can feel like a sign of weakness. However, setting boundaries and asking for help when you need it can actually be a sign of strength, as it shows that you are self-aware and in touch with your own needs.

Ultimately, finding a balance between independence and dependence is a lifelong journey. It requires self-reflection, self-awareness, and a willingness to be vulnerable with others. But with time, patience, and practice, you can cultivate a sense of autonomy while also building strong, meaningful relationships with those around you.

NAVIGATING THE CHALLENGES OF INTIMACY AND PARTNERSHIP

Intimacy and partnership are essential aspects of a fulfilling life, but they can also present unique challenges for women with Asperger's syndrome. If you're an adult woman with Asperger's, you may have struggled to navigate the complexities of romantic relationships, friendships, and even familial connections.

One of the key challenges in intimacy and partnership for women with Asperger's is striking the right balance between independence and dependence. On the one hand, you may value your independence and feel uncomfortable with the idea of relying on others. On the other hand, you may crave the emotional connection and support that a partner or close friend can provide.

It's important to understand that finding the right balance between independence and dependence is a journey that may take time and patience. You may need to experiment with different approaches and strategies to see what works best for you.

One important step in navigating the challenges of intimacy and partnership is to communicate openly and honestly with your partner or potential partner. Let them know what you need and what you struggle with, and ask for their support and understanding. This can be a vulnerable and difficult conversation to have, but it can also be a powerful way to build a stronger, more fulfilling relationship.

Another key aspect of navigating intimacy and partnership is to recognize and respect your own boundaries. It's okay to say no to things that feel uncomfortable or overwhelming, and to communicate your boundaries clearly and assertively. This can help you feel more in control of your own life and relationships, and can also help you build trust and respect with others.

Ultimately, navigating the challenges of intimacy and partnership as an adult woman with Asperger's is about finding the right balance between independence and dependence, and communicating openly and honestly with those around you. With time, patience, and support, you can learn to embrace your unique traits, overcome challenges, and thrive in all aspects of your life.

BUILDING HEALTHY BOUNDARIES AND ASSERTIVENESS SKILLS

One of the key challenges that many individuals with Asperger's Syndrome face is navigating social interactions, including setting appropriate boundaries with others. You may find that you struggle to assert yourself in relationships, whether with friends, family members, or romantic partners. This can be particularly challenging if you tend to be a people-pleaser or have difficulty saying no to others.

Building healthy boundaries and assertiveness skills is essential for maintaining healthy relationships and ensuring that your needs are met. It can also help you to feel more confident and in control of your life. But, I know it can be overwhelming to know how to begin this journey.

The first step in developing healthy boundaries and assertiveness skills is to take a deep dive into your inner self and identify your needs and values. This means taking the time to reflect on what truly matters to you in your relationships with others. What are your deal-breakers? What are the things that you need and want in a relationship? It's okay to feel vulnerable and uncertain at this stage, but remember that this process will help you to build stronger, more fulfilling connections in the long run.

Once you have a clearer sense of your needs and values, you can begin to communicate them assertively to others. This may involve setting clear boundaries around what you will and will not tolerate in your relationships. It may also involve speaking up for yourself and expressing your needs and desires in a clear and direct manner.

Finding Balance and Fulfillment in Relationships

It's natural to desire companionship and connection, but it's important to approach relationships in a way that feels comfortable and authentic to you.

At times, it may feel overwhelming to navigate the nuances of social interaction and communication. Many others with Asperger's Syndrome face similar struggles in their relationships. And just like any other aspect of life, it takes practice and patience to improve.

Finding meaningful relationships can be challenging, but it's important to stay true to your values and interests. When you connect with people who share your passions, you can experience a sense of belonging and fulfillment. Remember to communicate openly and honestly with your loved ones, and don't hesitate to express your thoughts and emotions. Healthy relationships require effort from both parties, so be prepared to compromise and show mutual respect. With time and dedication, you can cultivate fulfilling relationships that bring joy and meaning to your life.

While it can be tempting to try to fit into societal norms, it's important to stay true to yourself. Embrace your unique traits and qualities, as they are what make you special. With time, patience, and self-acceptance, you can find balance and fulfillment in your relationships, and live a fulfilling and happy life.

CHAPTER 11

COPING WITH LIFE'S UPS AND DOWNS

Navigating transitions and changes can be a daunting task for anyone, but it can be especially challenging for those with Asperger's Syndrome. As an adult woman with Asperger's, you may find yourself struggling to cope with the unexpected twists and turns that life can throw your way. However, with the right strategies and support, you can learn to manage these transitions and even thrive in the face of change.

One of the most important things to remember when facing a transition is to be kind to yourself. Change can be difficult, and it's normal to feel overwhelmed or anxious during times of transition. Allow yourself time to process your emotions and feelings, and don't be afraid to reach out for help or support when you need it.

Another helpful strategy for managing transitions is to create a plan of action. Identify the steps you need to take to navigate the change, and break them down into manageable tasks. This can help you feel more in control and less overwhelmed as you work through the transition.

It's also important to remember that transitions are a natural part of life, and they can often lead to new opportunities and experiences. Try to focus on the positive aspects of the transition, and keep an open mind to new possibilities that may arise.

There are many resources and support systems available to help you navigate transitions and changes in your life. Whether it's seeking out the advice of a therapist or support group, or simply talking to a trusted friend or family member, reaching out for help is a sign of strength, not weakness.

As a woman with Asperger's, you have already shown incredible resilience and strength in navigating the challenges of life with this condition. With the right strategies and support, you can continue to thrive in the face of change and manage transitions with confidence and grace.

EMBRACING FLEXIBILITY AND RESILIENCE

The rigidity of thought patterns and difficulty adjusting to new situations can make transitions and change feel overwhelming and anxiety-inducing.

One of the keys to navigating transitions and change is to embrace flexibility and resilience. This means being open to new possibilities and ways of doing things, and developing the ability to bounce back from setbacks.

One strategy for building flexibility and resilience is to practice mindfulness and meditation. These practices can help you become more aware of your thoughts and emotions, and develop a sense of calm and inner strength that can help you weather challenging situations.

It can also be helpful to create a support network of family, friends, and professionals who can provide encouragement and guidance during times of transition and change. This might include seeking the help of a therapist or counselor who can work with you to develop coping strategies and navigate the challenges of transition.

Always keep in mind that transitions and changes are a normal part of life. It is important to cultivate flexibility and resilience to face these obstacles with courage and determination. You can nurture these qualities by taking care of yourself, asking for help when needed, and being open to new opportunities. By doing so, you can develop the strength and adaptability to thrive in a world that is always evolving.

FINDING PEACE AND JOY IN THE JOURNEY

Life is full of transitions and changes, and for women with Asperger's Syndrome, these changes can be especially challenging. But as you navigate through these transitions, it's important to remember that finding peace and joy in the journey is possible.

Change can be overwhelming, whether it's a new job, a move to a new city, or a shift in your personal life. As someone with Asperger's Syndrome, you may feel a heightened sense of anxiety and stress in these situations. However, with the right tools and mindset, you can learn to embrace these changes and find happiness along the way.

One of the keys to finding peace and joy in the journey is to focus on the present moment. Rather than getting lost in worries about the future or regrets about the past, try to stay grounded in the here and now. Mindfulness practices, like meditation and deep breathing exercises, can be incredibly helpful in this regard.

Another important aspect of finding peace and joy in the journey is to cultivate a sense of gratitude. Even in the midst of difficult transitions, there are always things to be thankful for. Whether it's the support of loved ones, the beauty of nature, or the simple pleasures of everyday life, take time to appreciate the blessings in your life.

CHAPTER 12

CELEBRATING YOUR ACCOMPLISHMENTS AND LOOKING TO THE FUTURE

As an adult with Asperger's Syndrome, you have likely faced countless challenges throughout your life. From struggling with social interactions and communication to feeling overwhelmed by sensory stimuli, navigating the world can be difficult and overwhelming at times. However, it's important to remember that you are not defined by your diagnosis. You are a unique individual with strengths and talents that deserve to be celebrated.

In this final chapter, we will discuss strategies for thriving as an adult woman with Asperger's Syndrome. We'll explore ways to celebrate your accomplishments and look towards the future with optimism and hope.

One important aspect of thriving is learning to embrace your unique traits. As someone with Asperger's Syndrome, you may possess a unique way of thinking and processing information. This can be a valuable asset in many areas of life, including creative pursuits, problem-solving, and attention to detail. Rather than trying to hide or suppress these traits, it's important to embrace them and recognize their value.

Another key to thriving is finding a supportive community. This can be a challenge for many individuals with Asperger's Syndrome, as social interactions may be difficult. However, there are many online and in-person communities that cater to individuals on the autism spectrum. By connecting with others who share similar experiences, you can find a sense of belonging and support that can be incredibly empowering.

It's also important to set goals and work towards them, even if they feel daunting at first. Whether it's pursuing a new hobby, going back to school, or pursuing a career path, setting achievable goals and taking small steps towards them can help you feel a sense of purpose and accomplishment.

As you move forward, it's important to acknowledge and celebrate your accomplishments, no matter how small they may seem. Every milestone, every step forward, is a cause for celebration. By recognizing your strengths and accomplishments, you can cultivate a sense of self-confidence and resilience that will serve you well in the future.

To sum up, it's possible to thrive as an adult with Asperger's Syndrome by having a positive outlook, utilizing effective techniques, and receiving proper assistance. It's crucial to keep in mind that your diagnosis does not define you. You are a resilient, capable, and exceptional person with boundless possibilities.

EMBRACING YOUR UNIQUE PATH AND JOURNEY

You are a beautiful and unique individual, and your journey with Asperger's Syndrome is no exception. It's essential to celebrate your differences and embrace your quirks, as they make you who you are. By accepting yourself fully, you can find a sense of peace and fulfillment in your life. Do not forget that you are not alone, and there is a community of individuals with Asperger's who share similar experiences and challenges.

It's easy to feel like you don't fit in or that you're constantly struggling to meet the expectations of others. But the truth is, you don't have to conform to anyone else's standards. You are allowed to be exactly who you are, and you deserve to be celebrated for it.

So, embrace your interests, your passions, and your idiosyncrasies. Follow your heart and chase your dreams with all the courage you can muster. Your journey may be different from others, but that doesn't mean it's any less valuable or important.

You are an exceptional individual with incredible strengths and talents that can make a huge impact in the world. Your unique perspective and insights can offer a fresh take on things that others may have never thought of before. So, don't be afraid to share your voice and your perspective with the world.

As you continue on your journey, know that there will be challenges and obstacles to overcome. But by embracing your unique path, you'll be better equipped to face these challenges head-on and come out stronger on the other side.

BUILDING A MEANINGFUL AND PURPOSEFUL LIFE

As someone who may have struggled with social interactions, sensory overload, and other challenges, it's easy to feel like you don't quite fit in with the world around you. But the truth is, your unique traits can be the foundation for a truly fulfilling life, one in which you can make a real impact on the world around you.

Discovering what you are passionate about and what truly interests you is an essential step towards creating a meaningful and fulfilling life. Always remember that your individual set of passions and interests define you as a person, and they can be a tremendous driving force in shaping the life you desire.

Don't shy away from exploring your interests and pursuing your passions, as they can bring a sense of fulfillment and happiness to your life. Allow yourself to embrace your uniqueness and express yourself fully, for it is through our passions that we discover our purpose and joy in life.

Once you've identified your passions, the next step is to find ways to incorporate them into your daily life. This may mean pursuing a career in a related field, volunteering in a related organization, or simply making time to engage in activities that you enjoy. Whatever the path may be, the key is to make sure that your passions are an integral part of your life and that you are actively working to nurture and grow them.

Of course, building a meaningful life isn't just about pursuing your own interests. It's also about finding ways to connect with others and make a positive impact on the world around you.

Perhaps most importantly, building a meaningful life requires a willingness to take risks and try new things. As someone with Asperger's Syndrome, it's natural to feel more comfortable with routine and predictability. But the truth is, growth and fulfillment often come from stepping outside of our comfort zones and exploring new opportunities. Whether it's trying a new hobby, taking on a new challenge at work, or simply making an effort to connect with new people, taking small steps outside of your comfort zone can lead to big rewards.

CONCLUSION

As we reach the end of this book, I want to leave you with a powerful call to action. It's time for all of us to come together and empower women with Asperger's Syndrome, creating a world that is more inclusive and accepting of neurodiversity.

Throughout this book, we have explored the unique challenges and strengths of adult women with Asperger's Syndrome. We've discussed strategies for managing sensory overload, navigating social situations, and embracing creativity and unique interests. But the work doesn't end here.

We need to continue to advocate for better understanding and support for women with Asperger's Syndrome. We must challenge the stereotypes and misconceptions that too often limit their opportunities and potential. We must demand equal access to education, employment, and healthcare, as well as a more inclusive and accepting society.

Imagine a world where neurodiversity is celebrated, where differences are embraced and valued, and where everyone has the opportunity to thrive. This is the world that we must strive towards.

But it's not just about changing the world. It's also about empowering yourself. I hope that this book has provided you with the tools, strategies, and insights you need to live a fulfilling and rewarding life as an adult woman with Asperger's Syndrome. Always keep in mind that you have tremendous potential and are capable of accomplishing extraordinary things. Your individual perspective and skillset are exceptional and carry immense value and significance.

So, as you move forward on your journey, I encourage you to continue exploring your interests, seeking out new opportunities, and connecting with others who share your experiences. Let's work together to create a community that celebrates diversity and encourages inclusion. Let's break down the barriers that prevent women with Asperger's Syndrome from achieving their full potential.

Thank you for taking the time to read this book and for your commitment to making a difference. Let's work together to create a brighter future for all women with Asperger's Syndrome.

If you enjoyed this book or received value from it in any way, then I'd like to ask you a favor: would you be kind enough to leave a review for this book on Amazon? It'd be greatly appreciated!

Printed in Great Britain
by Amazon

24747090R00056